Kingdom Kidz Bible

with envelope surprises!

King Solomon

1 Kings 3:5–15; 10:1–10

PROMISE
PRESS

An Imprint of Barbour Publishing

When King David was too old to be king anymore, his son Solomon was crowned king. What a happy day!

In a dream, God told King Solomon to ask for anything he wanted. What did King Solomon ask for? He asked for wisdom!

"God, please give me Your wisdom," King Solomon said, "so I can be a good king and help Your people."

God was happy with what King Solomon said. "I will give you My wisdom," God said. "I will make you the wisest person in the whole wide world! And because you didn't ask for money or power, I will also give you riches and make you very, very famous."

Sure enough, King Solomon became the most famous person in the world. He became the richest person in the world. He became the wisest person in the world! King Solomon used God's wisdom to help people and to do good things.

People traveled from far and near just to ask King
Solomon questions and see how wise he really was.
One day the Queen of Sheba came from far away to visit
King Solomon.

The Queen of Sheba saw King Solomon's gold and riches. She asked him many questions. When she was ready to go back home, she gave him beautiful jewels and treasures from her own country. She said, "With God's wisdom, King Solomon is truly the wisest person in all the world!" King Solomon used God's wisdom to help people and to do good things.

I'm glad God is wise. He knows EVERYTHING. Today I pray, **Dear God, thank You for being wise. Amen.**